Peter Ilyitch Tchaikovsky

SYMPHONIES
Nos. 1, 2 and 3

IN FULL SCORE

DOVER PUBLICATIONS, INC.
NEW YORK

This Dover edition, first published in 1992, is a republication of three works originally published separately:

Pervaĭa simfoniĭa (g-moll) "Zimnie grĭozy" dlĭa bol'shovo orkestra / Première Symphonie (sol-mineur) "Rêverie d'hiver" pour grand orchestre; Vtoraĭa simfoniĭa (c-moll) dlĭa bol'shovo orkestra / Deuxième Symphonie (ut-mineur) pour grand orchestre and *Tret'ĭa simfoniĭa (D-dur) dlĭa bol'shovo orkestra / Troisième Symphonie (Re-majeur) pour grand orchestre,* all published by Gosudarstvennoe Muzykal'noe Izdatel'stvo / Editions de Musique de l'URSS, Moscow and Leningrad, 1946; edited by Igor Belza.

Library of Congress Cataloging-in-Publication Data

Tchaikovsky, Peter Ilich, 1840–1893.
    [Symphonies, no. 1–3]
    Symphonies nos. 1, 2, and 3 / Peter Ilyitch Tchaikovsky. — In full score.
    1 score.
    Reprint. Originally published: Moscow : Editions de musique de l'URSS, 1946.
    Contents: g-Moll — c-Moll — D-Dur.
    ISBN-13: 978-0-486-27050-0
    ISBN-10: 0-486-27050-5
    1. Symphonies—Scores.
M1001.C44 no. 1–3 1992   91-760342
                                              CIP
                                              M

Manufactured in the United States by R.R. Donnelley
27050508   2015
www.doverpublications.com

CONTENTS

Symphony No. 1 in G Minor, Op. 13

("Winter Daydreams")

SYMPHONY NO. 1

INSTRUMENTATION

Piccolo [Fl. picc.]

2 Flutes [Flauti, Fl.]

2 Oboes [Oboi, Ob.]

2 Clarinets (B♭) [Clarinetti in B, Cl.]

2 Bassoons [Fagotti, Fag.]

4 Horns (F, B♭) [Corni in F, Es; Cor.]

2 Trumpets (D, C) [Trombe in D, C; Trbe.]

2 Tenor Trombones [Tromboni tenore, Trbni.]

Bass Trombone [Trombone basso, Trbne. basso]

Tuba [Tba.]

Timpani [Timp.]

Cymbals [Piatti]

Bass Drum [Gran Cassa, Gr. C.]

Violins I,II [Violini, Viol.]

Violas [Viole]

Cellos [Violoncelli, Celli]

Basses [Contrabassi, C.-B.]

I.

Symphony No. 1 (I) / 7

Poco più animato

P **Poco più animato**

II. "Gloomy land, misty land"

III. Scherzo

IV. Finale

Allegro moderato ♩= 126
Fl. picc.
Fl.
a 2
f
Ob.
mf
Cl. in A
mf
Fag.
a 2
mf
f
a 2
Cor.
a 2
mf
mf
mf
Trbe.
mf
Viol. I
mf
mf
mf
sempre cresc.
mf
sempre cresc.
f
mf
sempre cresc.
f
Allegro moderato ♩= 126

Allegro maestoso ♩=126

Andante lugubre

Andante lugubre

Symphony No. 2 in C Minor, Op. 17

("Little Russian")

SYMPHONY NO. 2

INSTRUMENTATION

Piccolo [Fl. picc.]

2 Flutes [Flauti, Fl.]

2 Oboes [Oboi, Ob.]

2 Clarinets (B♭, C) [Clarinetti in B, C; Cl.]

2 Bassoons [Fagotti, Fag.]

4 Horns (F) [Corni in F, Cor.]

2 Trumpets (C) [Trombe in C, Trbe.]

2 Tenor Trombones [Tromboni tenore, Trbni. ten., Trbni.]

Bass Trombone [Trombone basso]
    (= Trombone III)

Tuba

Timpani [Timp.]

Cymbals [Piatti]

Bass Drum [Gran Cassa, Gr. Cassa, Gr. C.]

Tam-tam

Violins I, II [Violini, Viol.]

Violas [Viole]

Cellos [Violoncelli, Celli]

Basses [Contrabassi, C.-B.]

I.

Andante sostenuto

Andante sostenuto

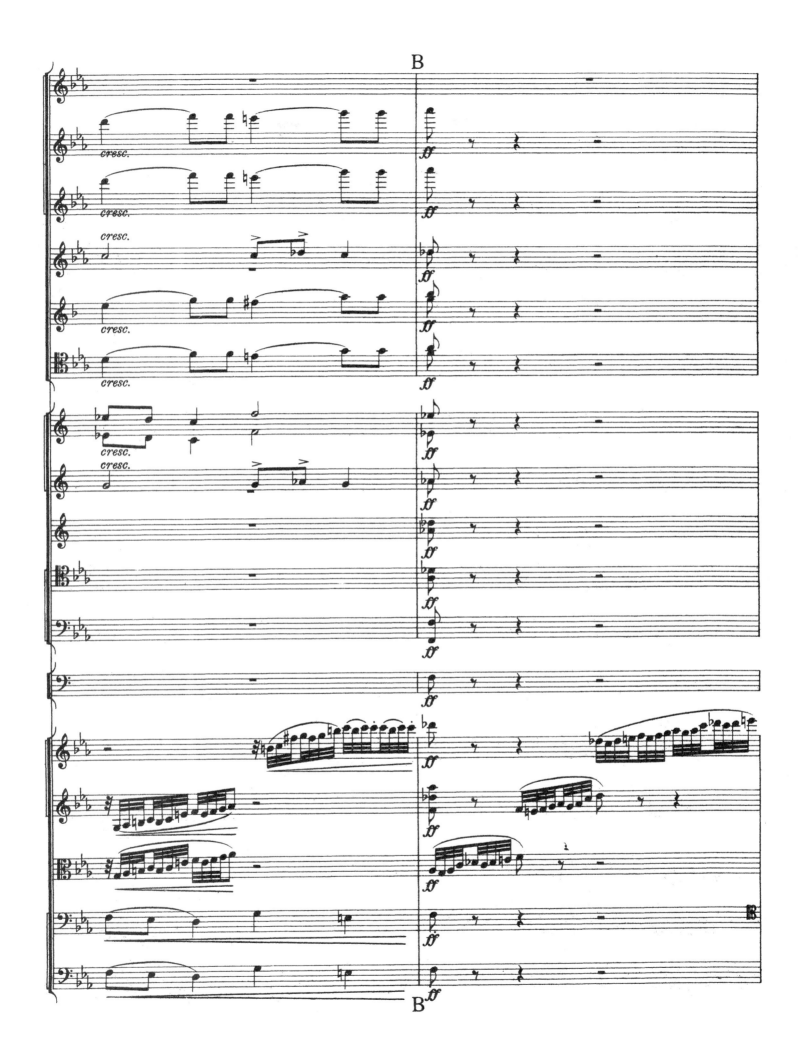

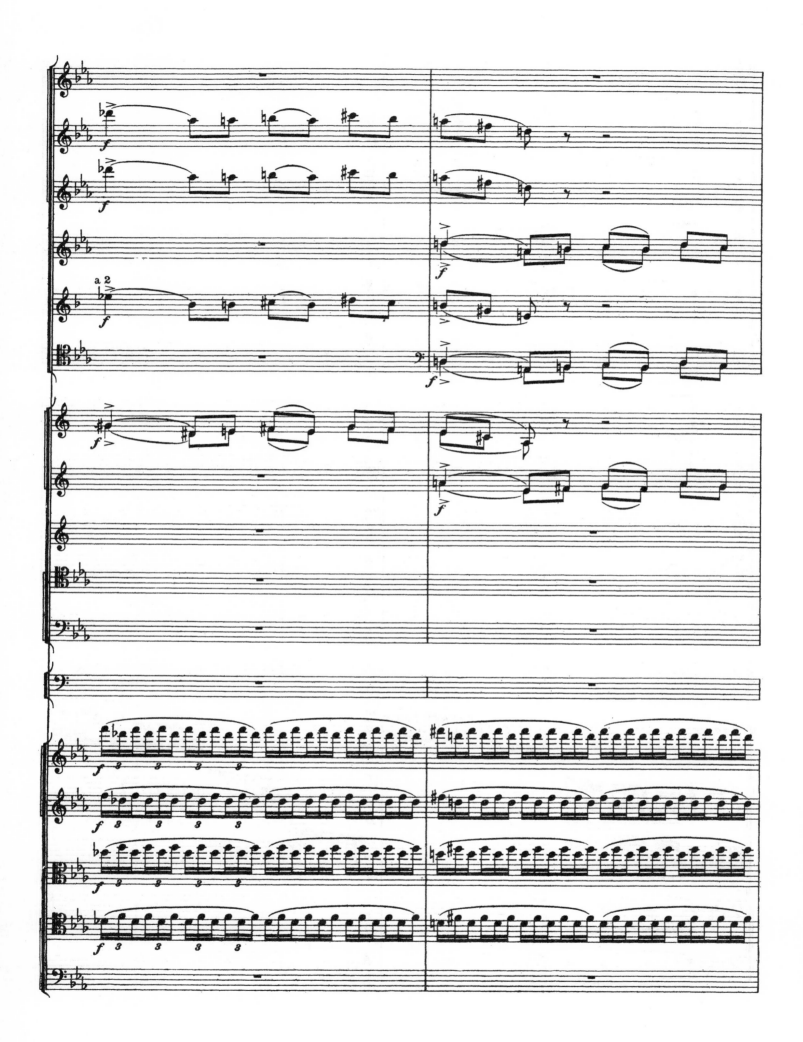

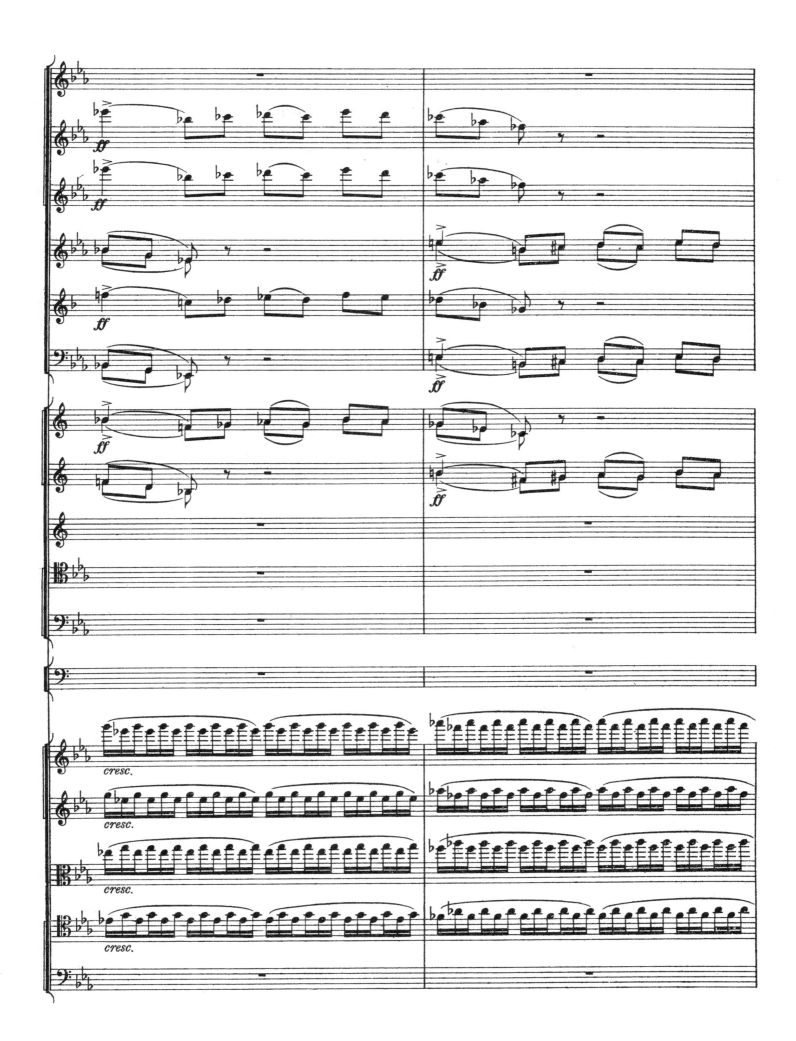

II.

III. Scherzo

Allegro molto vivace

Allegro molto vivace

IV. Finale

Allegro vivo

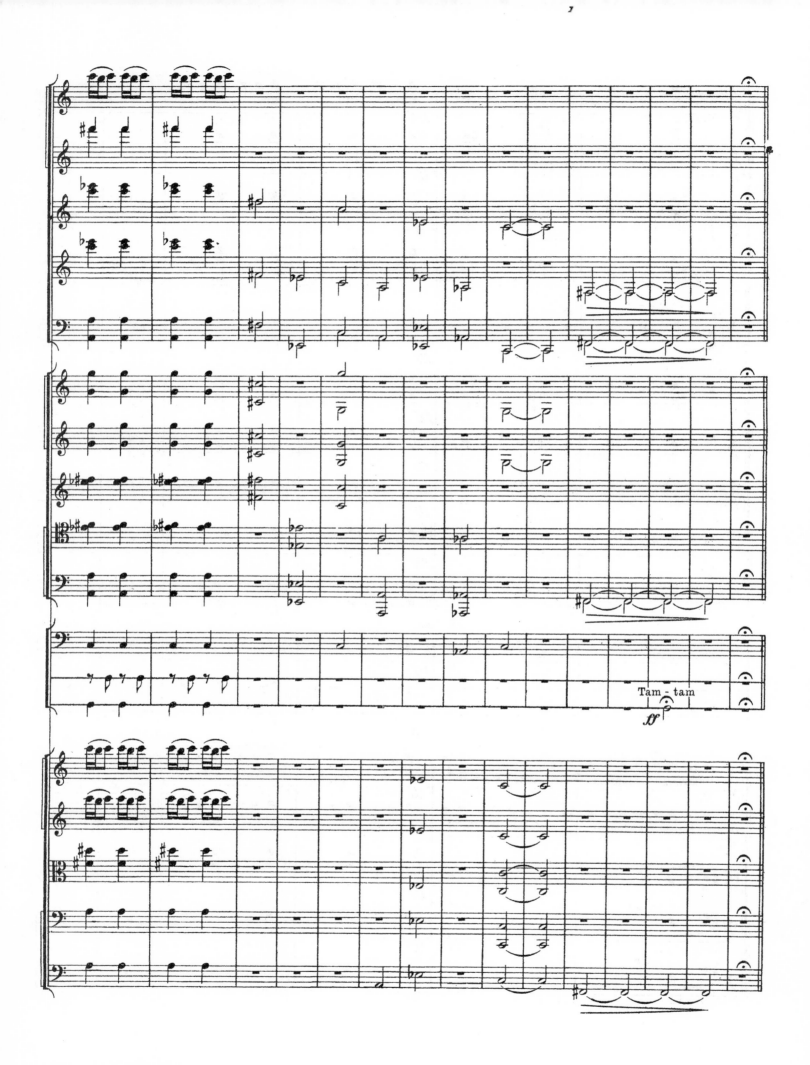

Symphony No. 3 in D Major, Op. 29
("Polish")

SYMPHONY NO. 3

INSTRUMENTATION

Piccolo [Picc.]

2 Flutes [Flauto, Fl.]

2 Oboes [Oboi, Ob.]

2 Clarinets (A, B♭) [Clarinetti in A, B; Cl.]

2 Bassoons [Fagotti, Fag.]

4 Horns (F) [Corni in F, Cor.]

2 Trumpets (F) [Trombe in F, Trbe.]

2 Tenor Trombones [Tromboni tenore, Trbni.]

Bass Trombone [Trombone basso, Trbne. III]

Tuba

Timpani [Timp.]

Violins I, II [Violini, Viol.]

Violas [Viole]

Cellos [Celli]

Basses [Contrabassi, C. Bassi, C.-B., Cb.]

I. Introduzione e Allegro

Molto più mosso

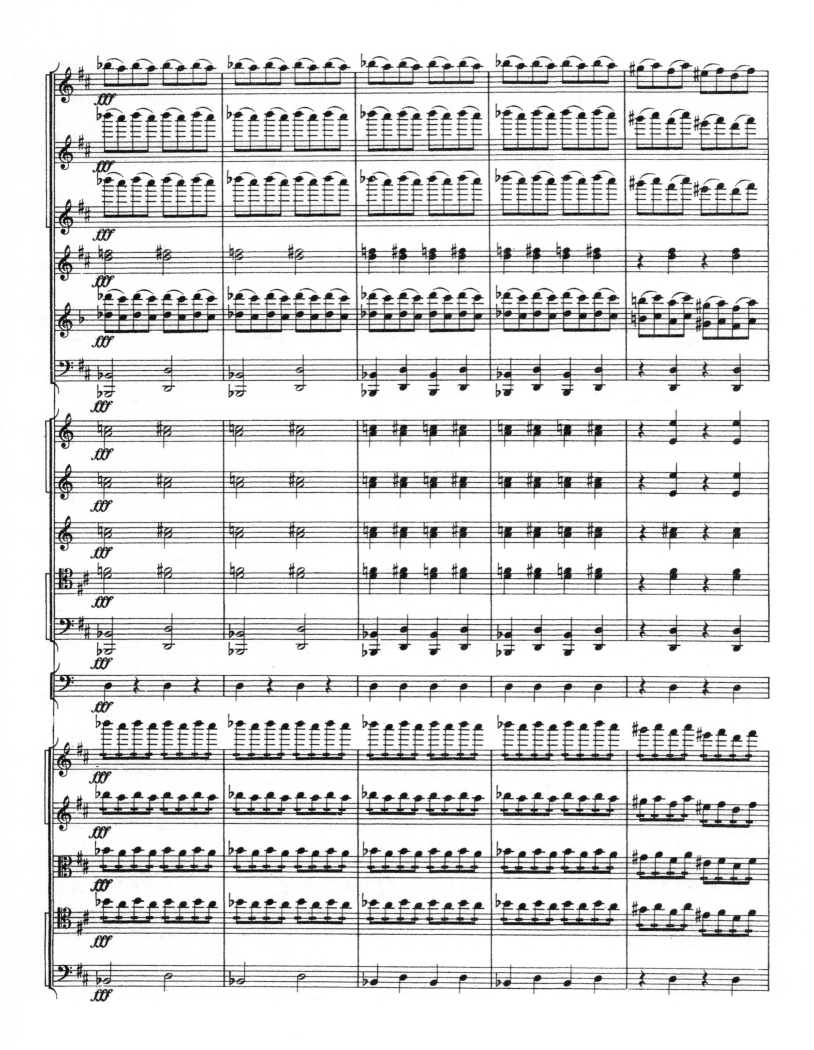

II. Alla tedesca

Trio
L'istesso tempo

L'istesso tempo

III. Andante

IV. Scherzo

V. Finale

Tempo I

Tempo I

Presto

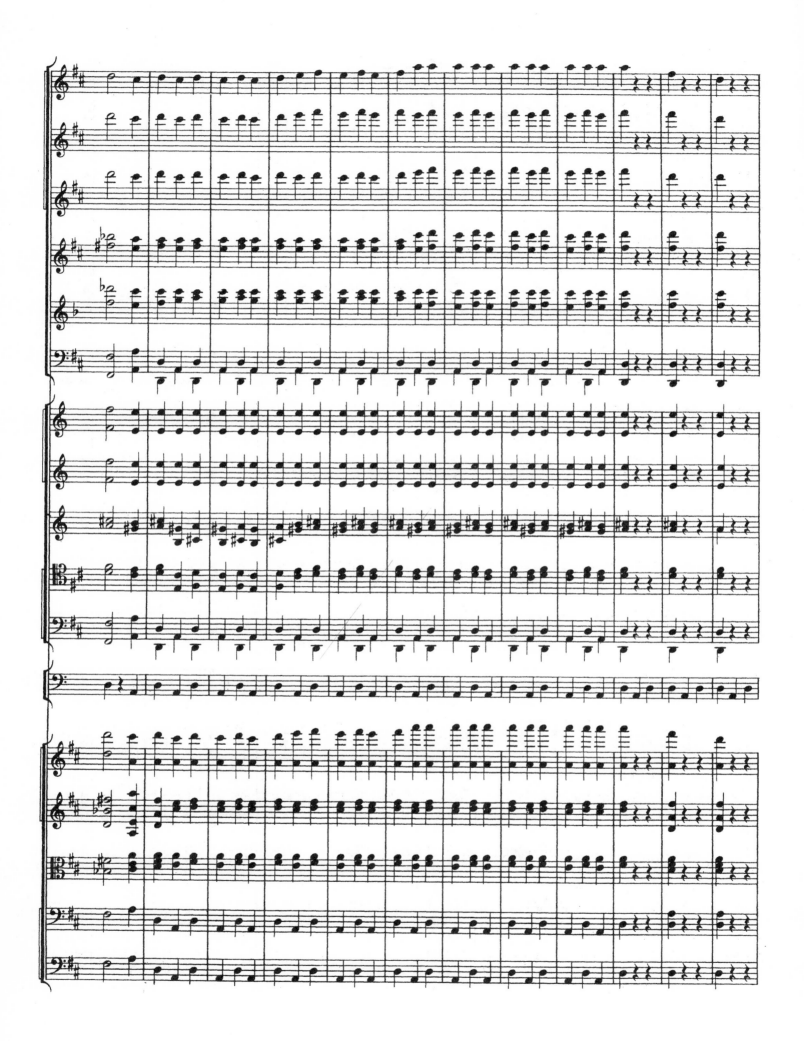

488 / Symphony No. 3 (V)

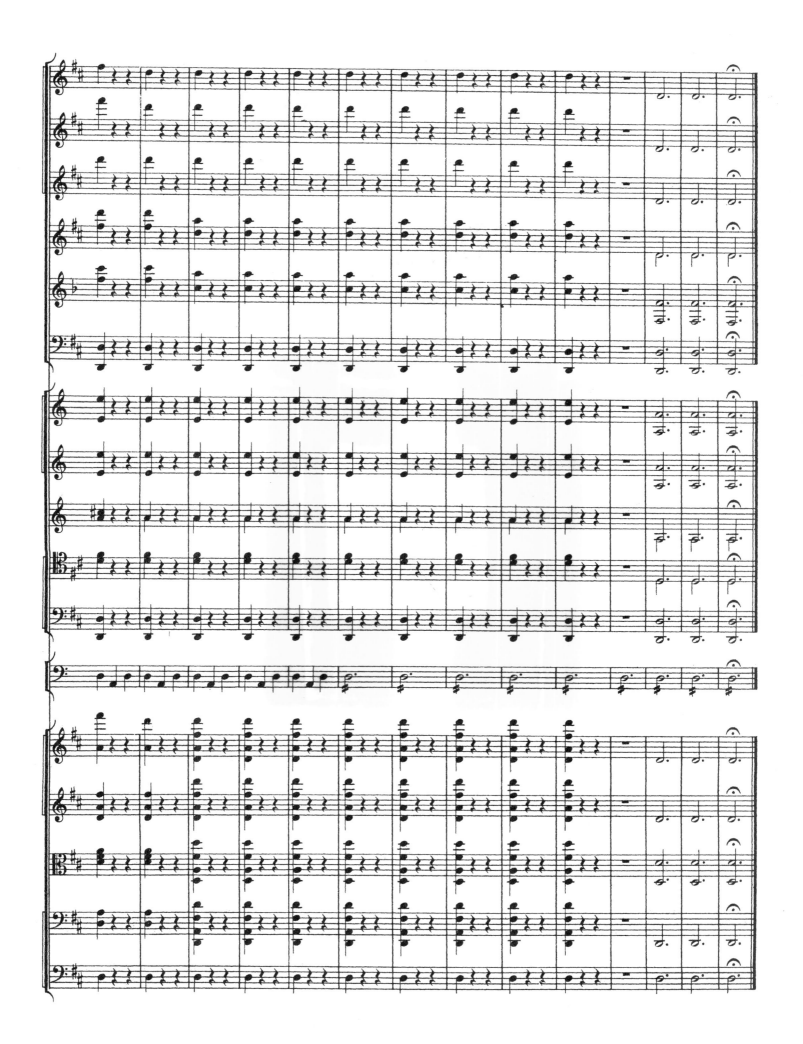